TRANSFORM

ELEVATE

THE POWER WITHIN

UNLEASH

By:TheSoulofMe

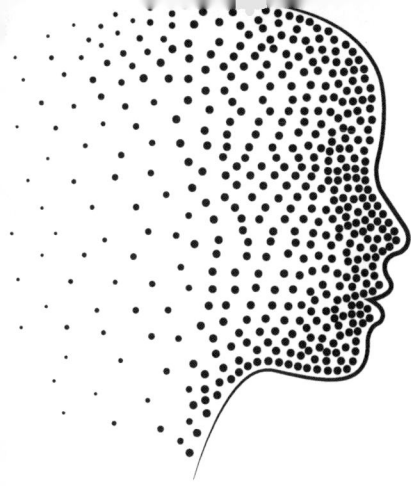

TRANSFORM

Transforming begins with a shift in mindset.

ELEVATE

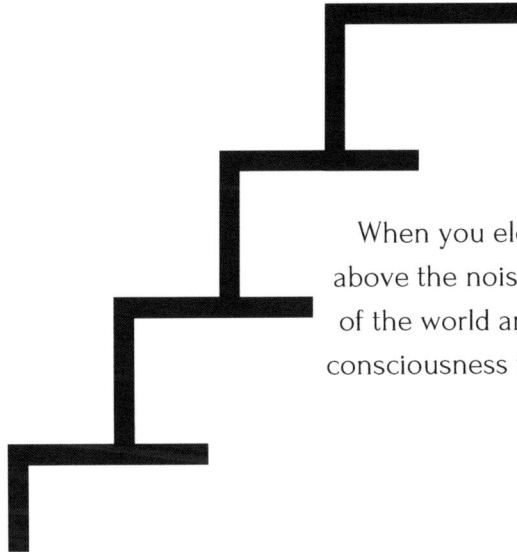

When you elevate, you rise above the noise and negativity of the world and awaken your consciousness to a higher level.

UNLEASH

By unleashing the power within, one can achieve their goals and dreams, and create a life that is truly fulfilling.

Meet Coach Emae

Edna McCants, more popularly known as Coach EMAE, is a Speaker, Master Life Coach, Author, and full-time Award-Winning Educator.

Edna "EMAE" McCants, CEO of "The Soul of Me." Her mission is to empower all women to unlock their full potential, overcome obstacles, and become their best selves. EMAE's life experiences have led her to believe that every woman has the innate strength to rise above societal norms and past traumas. Through her coaching, women are given the tools to transform, elevate, and unleash their inner power to move forward confidently toward being their authentic selves

transform

transform

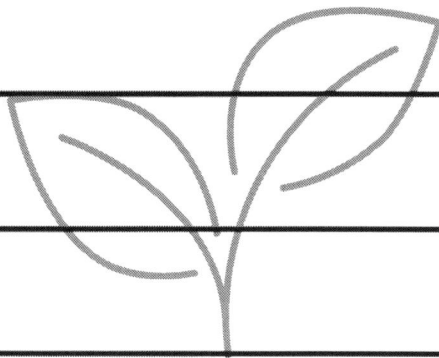

i trust my intuition and make choices that align with my highest good.

_____

_____

_____

_____

transform

_____

_____

_____

_____

TSM

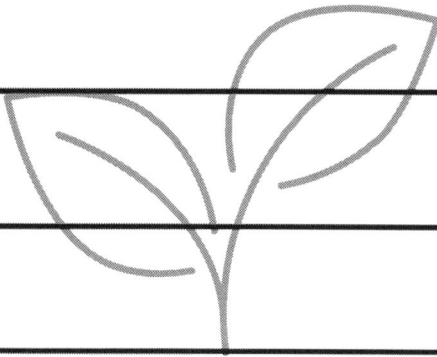

i am resilient; and every challenge i face only makes me stronger.

_____

_____

_____

_____

_____

transform

_____

_____

_____

_____

_____

i embrace change as an opportunity for growth and self-improvement.

_____

_____

_____

_____

_____

transform

_____

_____

_____

_____

_____

TSM

_____

_____

_____

_____

_____

transform

_____

_____

_____

_____

_____

_____

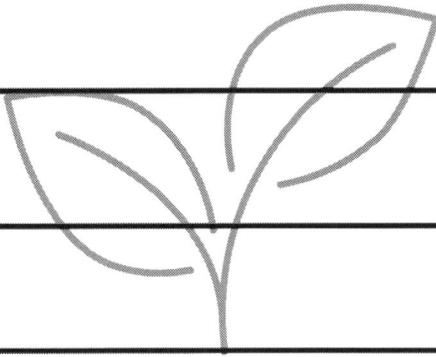

i am worthy of love; success; and all the blessings life has to offer.

_____

_____

_____

_____

_____

transform

_____

_____

_____

_____

_____

_____

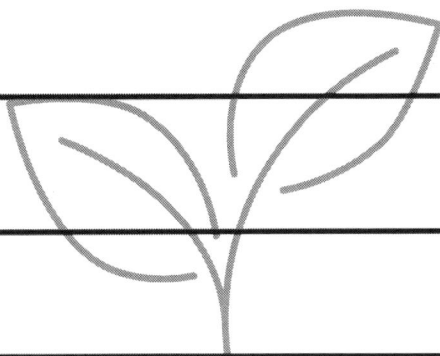

i celebrate my uniqueness and refuse to compare myself to others.

_____

_____

_____

_____

_____

transform

_____

_____

_____

_____

_____

TS&M

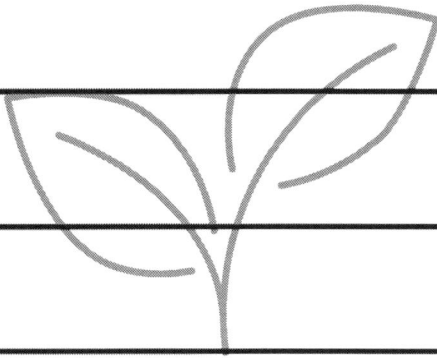

my mind is powerful; and i fill it with positivity and belief in my dreams.

_____

_____

_____

_____

transform

_____

_____

_____

_____

_____

TSM

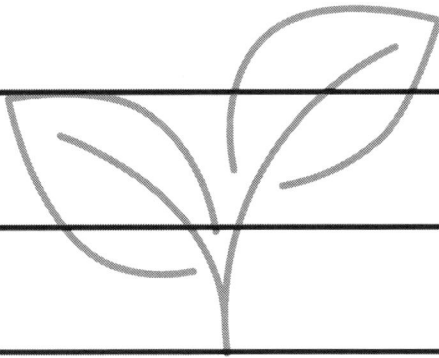

i am in control of my life and create my own happiness.

transform

i release self-doubt and welcome self-compassion and self-love.

transform

TSM

i attract positive energy; abundance; and supportive people into my life.

transform

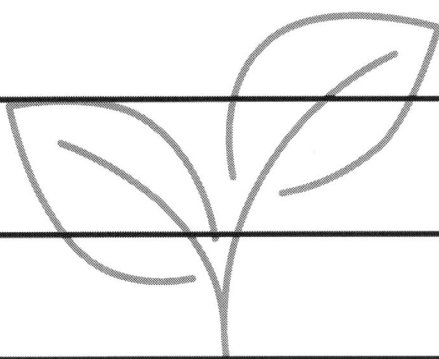

my past does not define me; i am constantly growing and evolving.

_____

_____

_____

_____

_____

transform

_____

_____

_____

_____

_____

TSM

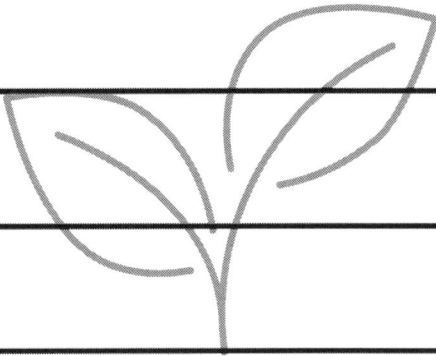

i honor my strengths and acknowledge my accomplishments; big and small.

transform

i am fearless in pursuing my goals and dreams.

transform

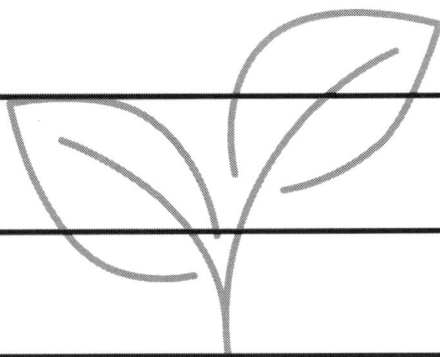

i am beautiful; both inside and out;
and i treat myself with kindness and respect.

transform

TSM

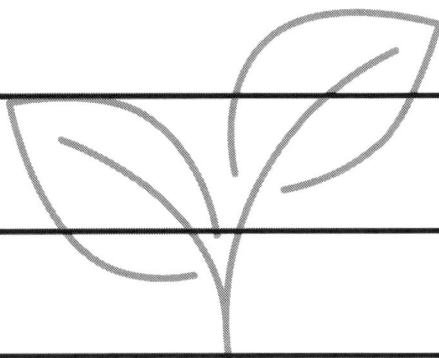

i am deserving of success; and i take purposeful steps toward my ambitions.

_____

_____

_____

_____

_____

transform

_____

_____

_____

_____

_____

TSM

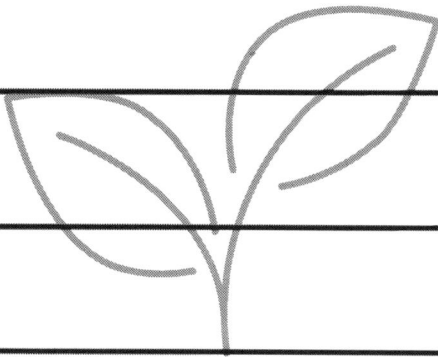

i speak my truth with courage and authenticity.

transform

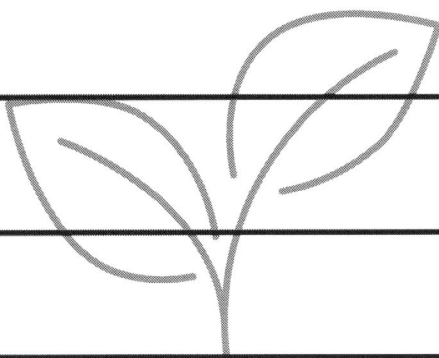

i am a source of inspiration and empowerment for those around me.

_____

_____

_____

_____

_____

transform

_____

_____

_____

_____

_____

TS&M

i embrace my journey of self-discovery;
and i am becoming the best version of myself each day.

_____

_____

_____

_____

transform

_____

_____

_____

_____

_____

i am a force of strength; grace; and empowerment.

elevate

TSM

my voice is powerful; and i use it to uplift and inspire.

_____

_____

_____

_____

_____

elevate

_____

_____

_____

_____

_____

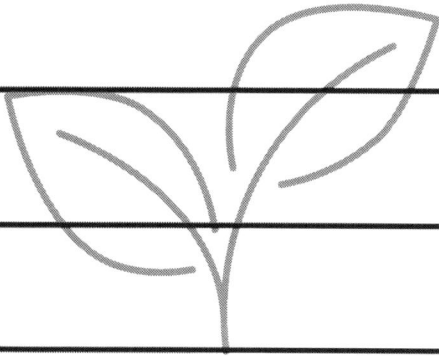

i am capable; competent; and equipped to handle any challenge that comes my way.

elevate

TSM

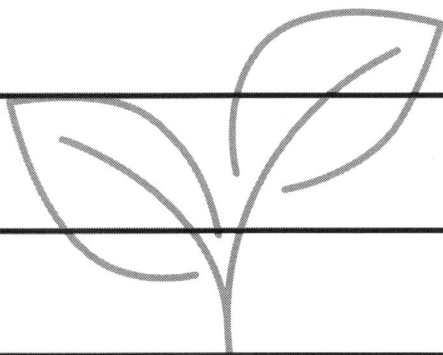

i walk confidently towards my goals and dreams; embracing my unique journey.

elevate

TSM

i am a beacon of positivity; radiating light and encouragement to those around me.

elevate

TSM

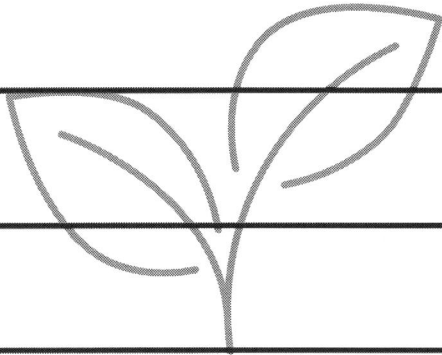

_____

_____

_____

_____

_____

elevate

_____

_____

_____

_____

_____

_____

TS&M

i am in charge of my destiny and create opportunities for success and growth.

elevate

i am a leader; guiding by example and fostering positive change.

elevate

TS&M

i believe in my abilities and trust the wisdom that resides within me.

elevate

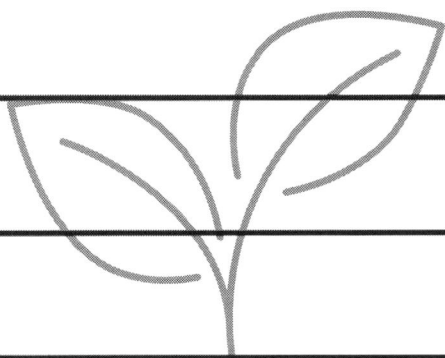

i honor my worth and recognize the strength in vulnerability and authenticity.

elevate

TSSM

i attract abundance and opportunities that align with my highest good.

elevate

TSM

i am a source of wisdom; love; and compassion in all my interactions.

elevate

TSM

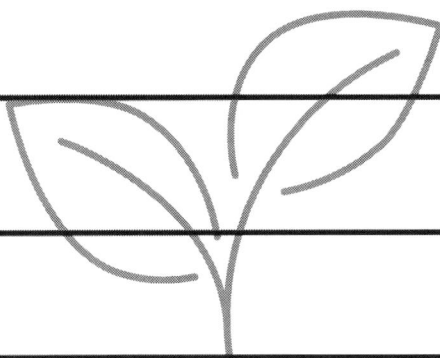

i embrace my uniqueness; knowing that my differences are my strengths.

elevate

TSM

elevate

TSM

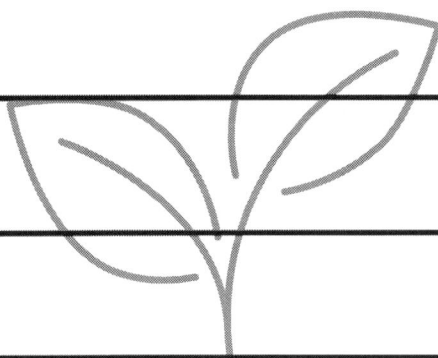

i choose to see challenges as opportunities for growth and learning.

elevate

TSM

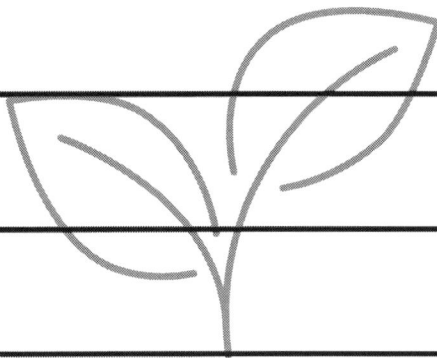

i am surrounded by a community that supports; uplifts; and celebrates my journey.

_____

_____

_____

_____

_____

elevate

_____

_____

_____

_____

_____

TSM

_____

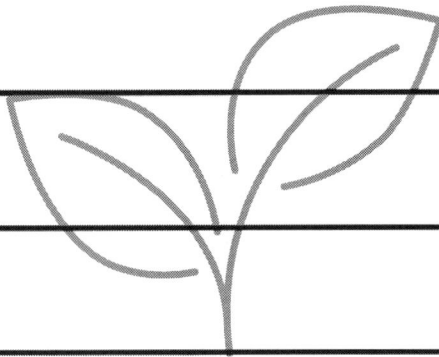

i step into each day with confidence; resilience; and an open heart.

elevate

TSM

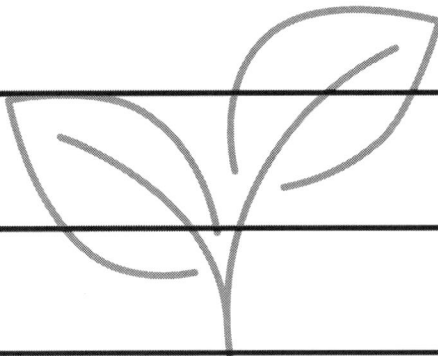

i am deserving of success; and i welcome it into my life with open arms.

elevate

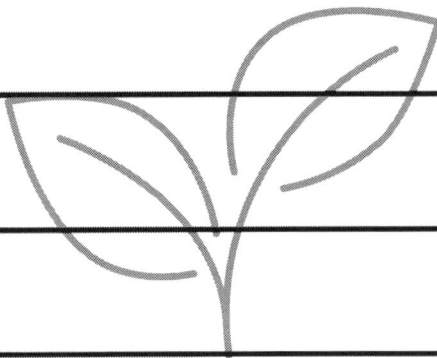

i am constantly evolving; expanding; and embracing my full potential.

_____

_____

_____

_____

elevate

_____

_____

_____

_____

_____

TSM

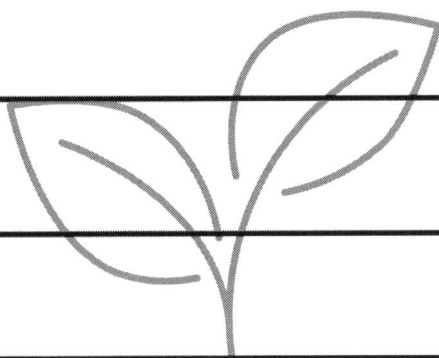

i am an empowered woman; and i lift others as i rise.

elevate

TSM

unleash

TSM

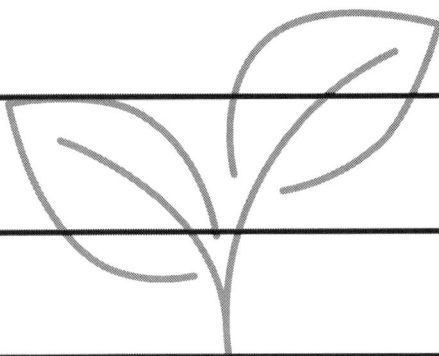

i am a reservoir of untapped potential and limitless strength.

unleash

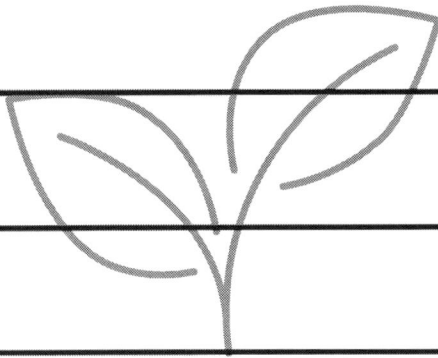

i embrace my unique abilities and allow them to shine brightly.

---

unleash

TSM

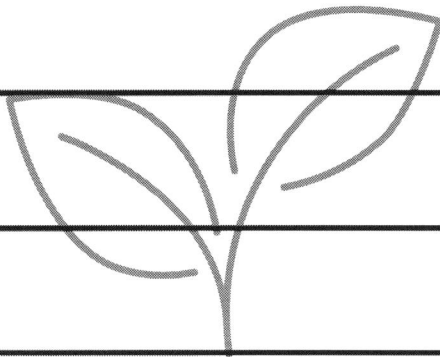

i am the architect of my destiny; sculpting my life with purpose and determination.

_____

_____

_____

_____

_____

unleash

_____

_____

_____

_____

_____

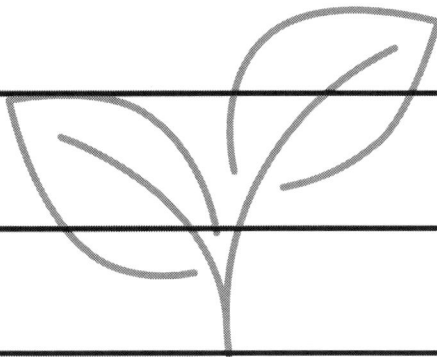

my inner strength propels me forward; overcoming any obstacle in my path.

unleash

TSM

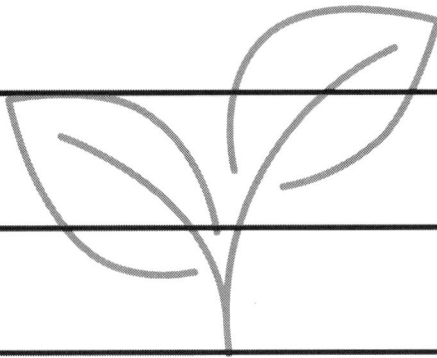

i am a warrior; channeling resilience and courage in every situation.

_____

_____

_____

_____

_____

unleash

_____

_____

_____

_____

_____

TSM

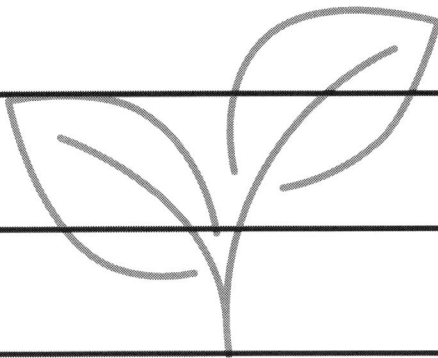

i am the master of my thoughts; choosing positivity and empowerment.

unleash

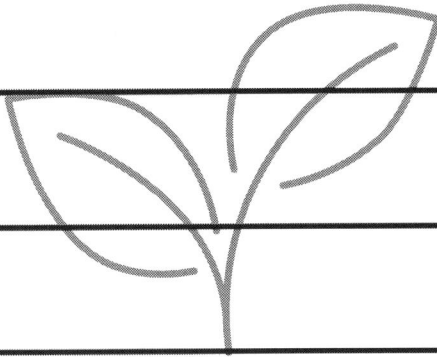

i am a magnet for success; attracting opportunities that align with my purpose.

_____

_____

_____

_____

_____

unleash

_____

_____

_____

_____

_____

_____

TS&M

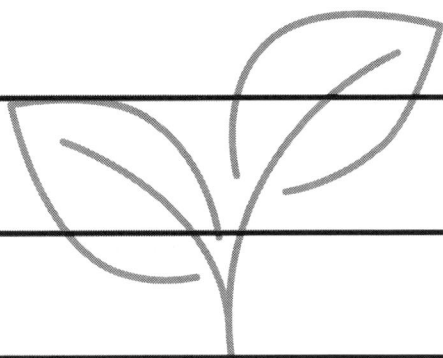

i am capable of creating positive change in my life and in the world around me.

_____

_____

_____

_____

_____

unleash

_____

_____

_____

_____

_____

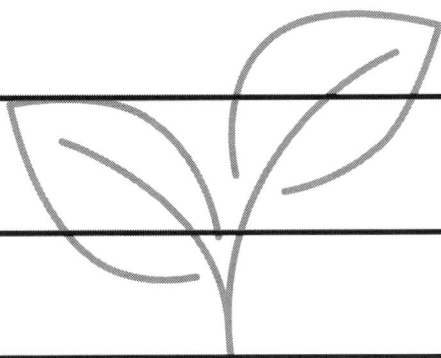

i trust my instincts and follow the guidance of my inner wisdom.

unleash

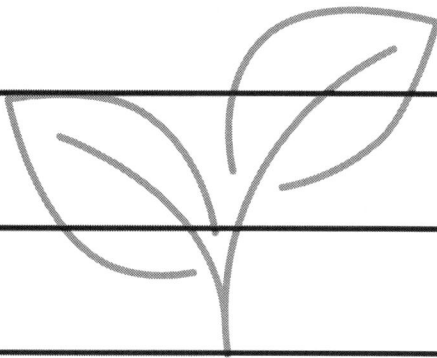

i release self-doubt and embrace the confidence that resides within me.

_____

_____

_____

_____

_____

unleash

_____

_____

_____

_____

_____

T8M

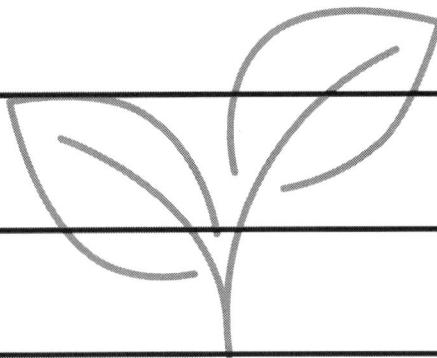

i celebrate my uniqueness and allow my authenticity to shine.

unleash

TS&M

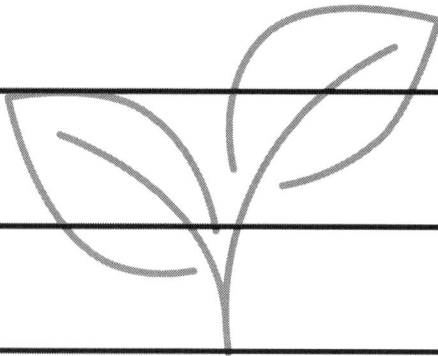

i am a source of inspiration; lighting the way for others to find their power.

_____

_____

_____

_____

_____

unleash

_____

_____

_____

_____

_____

_____

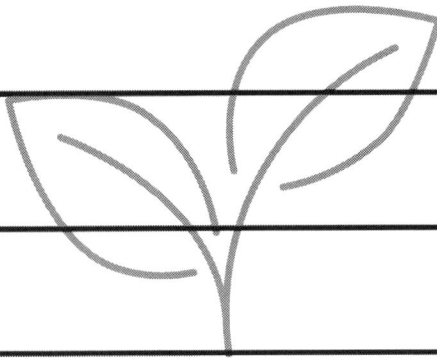

i am the author of my story; writing chapters filled with resilience and triumph.

unleash

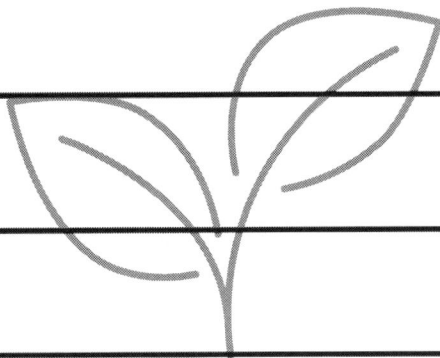

i embrace challenges as opportunities to showcase my strength and growth.

unleash

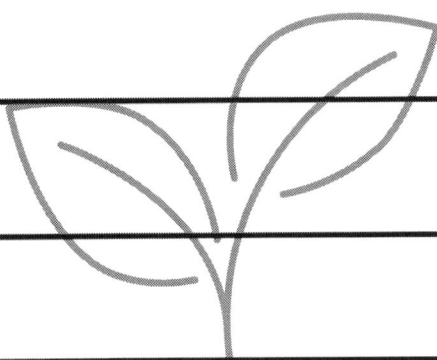

i am a wellspring of creativity; innovation; and potential.

_____

_____

_____

_____

_____

unleash

_____

_____

_____

_____

_____

i empower myself by empowering those around me; fostering a community of strength.

---

unleash

TS&M

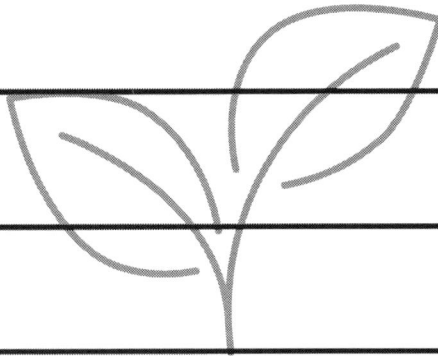

i am unstoppable; conquering hurdles with grace; determination; and resilience.

unleash

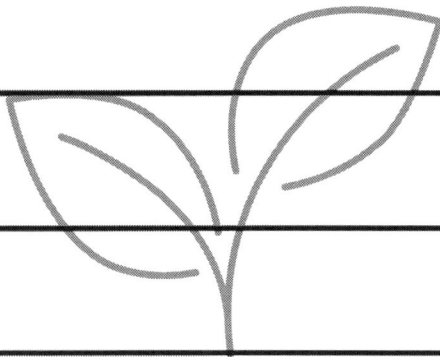

i radiate self-love and acceptance; nurturing the power within.

unleash

TS&M

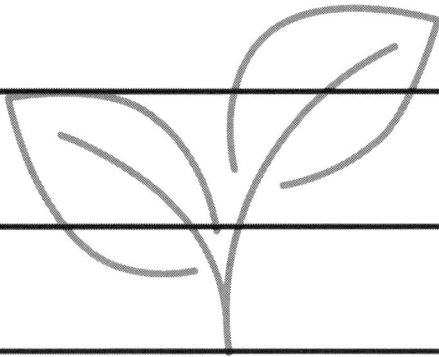

i unleash the force of my inner strength;
embodying empowerment in every step i take.

unleash

TSM

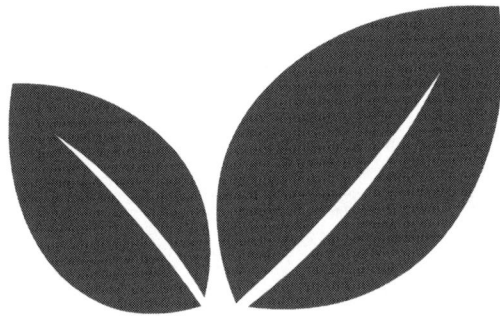

The Journey Begins Within

Made in the USA
Coppell, TX
28 October 2024

39260477R00072